FAMILY CIRCUS

I JUST DROPPED GRANDMA!

To mommy!

Have a very merry
Christmas and
a happy new
year!!

Bil Keane

Love,
Jason

FAWCETT GOLD MEDAL • NEW YORK

"I'm mailing you a letter, Grandma.
Wanna hear what it says?"

"No fair! She's tellin' grandma
all the things I was gonna
tell her!"

"I'm getting tired. Instead of a wishing
well, let's have a wishing puddle."

"I can't find Jeffy anywhere.
We'll go look for him as soon
as I finish making his bed."

"Better take these cars with you.
This is a tow-away zone."

"Look, Mommy! That chair has a leg like your wine glasses."

"The ice cream keeps tryin'
to escape."

"Mommy's head aches because of
a science infection."

"Go get some ice cubes, and
we'll play Titanic."

"Could you blow up our air mattress?
It's out of breath."

"Look, Mommy! These magic markers
can make each fingernail
a different color."

"If everybody eats a peck of dirt
during a lifetime, I think PJ must
be 'bout ready to go."

"When they invented dinner I wish
they'd put dessert up front."

"I'm not banging on anything. I'm just drying my baseball."

"San Francisco had a big earthquake
when Mrs. O'Leary kicked over a
lantern at the Cow Palace."

"This is the same stuff we saw in
Philadelphia, only here they
say 'San Francisco.' "

"Mommy! Jeffy said a naughty
word, 'FRISCO'!"

"Is it all held up with just those strings?"

"If you drop that ball, Jeffy, Daddy will
have to fish it out of the ocean."

"No, that's Alcatraz. Hawaii is further out."

"Can we get pizza for lunch?"

"We'll never get up any speed if that guy doesn't stop pulling on the brake!"

"Why do they call it a cable car?
I didn't see any TV."

"I thought Fisherman's Wharf was a
place we could fish off of."

"Is that the fish I smell or the bait?"

"Will they give us a kitty bag?"

"I didn't know they made tricycles
for grownups!"

"If I'd known about all these hills, I would
have brought my skateboard."

"You better be good, PJ, or you'll
land in solitary."

"The break is set for midnight. Bring
your snorkel. Pass it on."

"Could we have Japanese SODAS
instead of tea?"

"FOG? I thought you said 'Look
at the FROG!' "

"PJ's not lookin' at the skyline, Mommy.
He's lookin' at his ice-cream cone."

"Is Labor Day when we start counting
how many days till Christmas?"

"I had a no-hitter going — till the bottom half of the second."

"Don't turtles ever get to go out and play?"

"The hardest part about flossin' is
trying not to lose your place."

"So how was your first week of school?"

"Fine, but I got laid off for two days."

"Grandma looked at the card I made her
and cried 'cause she was touched.
But I didn't touch her, honest!"

"We went to your house yesterday,
but we couldn't find you."

"I wonder if anybody is holding auditions for detergent commercials."

"All right for you, Jeffy! You'll never
grow up to be a Mr. Rogers!"

"But my brain isn't hungry."

"Know what, Mommy? I have three
kinds of brothers — big brother,
kid brother and baby brother."

"Are we going to have an indoor
pool for the winter?"

"You're wasting it. Mommy
went outside."

"One more time I am going to demon-
strate how to put a top
back on a jar."

"Doesn't it have a pretty lawn?"

"Daddy said his car needs a
new battery."

"Hi, Grandma. Guess what came out."

"Come eat your lunch. HIKE!"

"If you're too sick to go to school,
mommy makes you stay sick all day."

"Why does Billy always get to
be the oldest?"

"He said to veer left at the light, Mommy.
Do you know how to veer?"

"It is NOT a magic trick! I'm
stuck to it with ice cream,
jelly and candy."

"PJ's tryin' to pet the fish."

"I can't reach my back. Is it okay if I
wash my front twice instead?"

"For the information of whoever's been adding to my grocery list, there's no 'K' in 'chocolate.' "

"There's a darn ol' fly in here and
I'm letting him out."

"Is that a fishing truck?"

"I suggest you transform yourself into
a student and do your homework."

"Oh good! Can we play store?"

"We have our own channel now."

"We learned about bones and teeth today.
Can I have a bowl of calcium?"

"This is the salt and this one is
the... um... the dirty salt."

"Winter's coming. Soup commercials
are back."

"When PJ was a tiny baby, why did
the priest at church put him
in a birdbath?"

"Chris brought his canary to see
your cuckoo clock."

"Hold up your goal posts, Daddy!"

"She's your only sister, and you'll
just have to LEARN
to like her."

"Are these socks brothers?"

"When you sneeze, are you s'posed
to say 'AHchoo!' or "KETCHoo!'?"

"Every time I turn on TV they're
showing a commercial."

"Oh boy! A lot more bags for
our bag collection!"

"Mommy, will you watch that pretty
red one, and save it for me
when it falls?"

"Would you get your camcorder, Daddy?
We want to make a video."

"Mommy, what time are my feet?"

"That's the jury, Jeffy,
not the choir."

"YOU may think of this as the
nuclear age, but to me it's
the paper towel age."

"Know what, Mommy? Crayons don't
erase so good."

"You call THAT a kiss?"

"Coloring books are full of ghosts that
you have to bring back to life."

"Skeletons aren't scary. Everybody
has one inside.

"Instead of dressing up, couldn't I go
as a civilian?"

"Let's postpone the trading until we
finish our rounds and get
back home."

"You don't have to make breakfast
for me, Mommy."

"The pictures show what happens in
the story, and the words
are the play-by-play."

"I don't like sending postcards.
The mailman can see your
spellin' mistakes."

"You were thinner then, Daddy. But
your tie was fatter.

"It isn't fair! The teacher and
the bus driver both make
me sit up front."

"You can't see our state. It
has clouds over it."

"I'm hungry."

"There, he's all clean. Don't try
to feed him any more honey."

"Are you going to bend down here,
Grandma, or shall I just
hug your legs?"

"Stop lookin' at it, Jeffy. Grandma
says a watched pot
never boils."

"Some night can I stay up and watch
the date change on
your watch?"

"I can spell 'mouse' — listen:
M...I...C...K...E...Y."

"Mommy, know what Billy's learnin'
from daddy? How to be a
couch potato."

"When it got cold they moved
to their winter home —
a fuzzy slipper."

"I like the way all the violinists
keep in step."

"What do we hafta have for dinner?"

"Don't eat the soup till it
gives up smoking."

"Stop jumping out, PJ! I can't keep
turnin' this plane around
to pick you up."

"Does our daily bread mean
crusts, too?"

"I am SO gettin' big! I'm almost
as tall as Michael J. Fox!"

"What date does this milk go bad?"

"Remember what daddy said, PJ. Eat
all your food or you'll be
sent to Africa."

"They're playing Christmas carols,
Mommy. Can we get our tree?"

"I wish we never had PJ!"

"You tell us never to shine a flash-
light in people's eyes, so how
come Dr. Flindall does it?"

"I can't wear these new jeans till
they learn to relax."

"Daddy, how do you spell 'ME'? And
say it one letter at a time."

"Sorry, our computer is down.
Please call tomorrow."

"Why does Kareem wear his swimmin'
goggles for basketball?"

"I wish oranges had a tab
you could pull."

"I don't think mommy wants you playing hide-and-seek in the..."

"Did she eat margarine?"

"We just accidentally mailed
a mitten."

"He doesn't talk anymore. I think
he needs a microchip transplant."

"Mommy, you don't have any money,
just dollars."

"I ran out of butter before I ran out
of toast."

"Is this where grandma gets the cards
with money in them?"

"Stop pouting before mommy SITS
on that lip."

"I expect you to bring back four
children and eight gloves."

"Have you been a good girl today?"

"Yes, and I'm tired out from it."

Medallion Island

SKERRIN

TOLKERRIN

CRANNOCH ISLES

THE TRINE

UTMOURN

WOLVADOR

PENMAR

TRUTHOON ISLES

GABROLIN

TRESKENNA

TRAU'MESTIS

LITTLE GU'LL

GU'LL ISLAND

MEDALLION ISLAND

THE CHAIN OF GOLDENISLE